Echoes BETWEEN LANGUAGES

Two Tongues, One Soul in Poems

MARTIN KARI

Copyright © 2025 Martin Kari.

All rights reserved. No part of this book may be reproduced, stored, or transmitted by any means—whether auditory, graphic, mechanical, or electronic—without written permission of both publisher and author, except in the case of brief excerpts used in critical articles and reviews. Unauthorized reproduction of any part of this work is illegal and is punishable by law.

ISBN: 978-1-63950-351-3 (sc)
ISBN: 978-1-63950-352-0 (hc)
ISBN: 978-1-63950-355-1 (e)

Because of the dynamic nature of the Internet, any web addresses or links contained in this book may have changed since publication and may no longer be valid. The views expressed in this work are solely those of the author and do not necessarily reflect the views of the publisher, and the publisher hereby disclaims any responsibility for them.

Writers Apex

Gateway Towards Success

8063 MADISON AVE #1252
Indianapolis, IN 46227
+13176596889
www.writersapex.com

Dedication

To **Arja Kari**

*You were the morning light
that warmed my days,
the quiet hand that steadied my journey,
the laughter that filled the
silence of ordinary hours.*

*Across oceans and continents
we walked together,
rooted in love,
raising children who carried
our joy forward,
building a home that was less a
place than a harmony of hearts.*

*Your patience taught me simplicity.
Your strength taught me trust.
Your love taught me what
it means to live fully.*

*Now you rest in a realm
my eyes cannot see,
yet I feel you in every breeze,*

*in the whisper of trees,
in the hush of twilight skies.
Even absence is not absence—
it is the shape of your presence
pressed into my soul.*

*This book bears your name
as much as mine,
for every page is touched by your spirit,
every word carries the echo
of our shared life,
every silence holds the
grace you left behind.*

*I write, I remember, I love—
not only for myself,
but for us,
for the two lives bound as one,
still walking, still whispering,
still eternal.*

Martin

LIST OF POEMS

About the Author vi

Preface viii

1. A Glorious Day 1
2. Joy of Writing 11
3. Nature's Cathedral 15
4. Dreams & Reality 31
5. Fire 35
6. Outback Journey in Australia 39
7. The Wheel Barrow 55
8. Love is Not Only a Word 59
9. Falling Leaves - Autumn 63
10. Winter (English) 69
11. Springtime 75
12. Summer 81
13. The Hand of Trust 87
14. About Life 93
15. Gone are the days 96
16. The Old House 105
17. Christmas 111
18. Religion is Poesy, Too 117

INHALTSVERZEICHNIS

Über den Autor vii

Vorwort ix

1. Ein Herrlicher Tag 3
2. Freude am Schreiben 13
3. Natur Kathedrale 17
4. Traum & Wirklichkeit 33
5. Feuer 37
6. Reise Ins Outback 41
7. Der Schubkarren 57
8. Die Liebe ist Nicht nur ein Wort 61
9. Fallende Blätter - Herbst 65
10. Winter (deutsch) 71
11. Frühling 77
12. Sommer 83
13. Die Hand des Vertrauens 89
14. So Läuft das Leben 95
15. Das Alte Haus 107
16. Weihnachten 113
17. Religion & Poesie 119

ABOUT THE AUTHOR

Born during World War II in Transylvania, Martin Kari undertook many directions in his life, starting as a refugee in Germany. Technical and then formal higher education prepared the author for life with a sense of exploration, adventure, intellect and humanity. Having worked and lived in four continents as a global citizen, he settled in Australia with his wife and six children. It was only in retirement that he found the time to take up the pen again.

ÜBER DEN AUTOR

Martin Kari wurde im Zweiten Weltkrieg in Siebenbürgen/Transylvanien als zweiter Sohn des Weinbauers Michael Lutsch Und seiner Frau Sara geboren. Der Autor folgte in seinem Leben Verschiedenen Wegen; ein Weg begann mit der Flucht seiner Adoptiv-Eltern nach Deutschland. Schul-Ausbildung, Technische- und Höhere Ausbildung bereiteten den Autor für ein Leben vor mit Entdeckungen, Abenteuer, Intellekt und Menschlichkeit. Der Autor hat in vier Kontinenten gelebt, gearbeitet und 1981 in Australien sich erfolgreich mit seiner finnischen Frau Arja, geborene Kari und ihren sechs Kindern niedergelassen. Im Alter von 65 Jahren verließ der Autor die „Berufliche-Tretmühle". Erst dann fand er zum ersten Mal Zeit, in seinem Leben die Schreibfeder wieder heraus zu holen. Gegenwärtig, bis ins Jahr 2017, habe ich soweit 24 Bücher in der deutschen Sprache und 24 Bücher in der englischen Sprache herausgebracht in sehr unterschiedlicher Thematik. Damit ist noch lange kein Ende erreicht, es geht weiter, solange es mir vergönnt bleibt. Es ist nie zu spät, etwas Neues im Leben zu beginnen; ist die Botschaft des Autors und seine Leser und Mitmenschen.

PREFACE

"The poet shows human power"
(Translation : Faust – Goethe)

"Poems of Martin Kari follow the form of prose poems. Prose poetry generally is written very much from the heart. It does not concern itself too much with form and line ending. It aims at telling the truth. His poems vary in length and are often written in story style. It does not try to be very clever, constantly inviting stress to find fresh metaphor. It tells what it wants to in plain language. The poet expresses a strong desire to share with the reader what he sees, how he feels. A classical sample for prose poetry out of the past would be the French poet Baudelaire (1821-1867), Paris). Martin Kari poems are however very much reflecting on a more modern understanding."

(From the FAWQ-Poetry Editor's Desk, Caroline Glen)

VORWORT

„Des Menschen Kraft im Dichter offenbart"
(Faust-Goethe)

„Die Gedichte von Martin Kari folgen der Prosa-Gedicht-Form. Prosa-Gedichte sind gewöhnlich vom Herzen geschrieben. Dabei kommt es nicht so sehr auf Form und wie die Zeilen auslaufen darauf an. Im Mittelpunkt steht die Wahrheit. Seine Gedichte unterscheiden sich auch in Länge, sie lehnen sich oft an Geschichts Erzählung an. Die Worte zielen nicht auf besonderen Intellekt, womit sie unausweichlich die Suche nach Vermittlung heraufbeschwören. Seine Gedichte sagen im Klartext aus, was am Herzen liegt. Der Dichter vermittelt dem Leser ein starkes Bedürfnis, zu erfahren, was die Augen gemeinsam ausfindig machen können und darüber hinaus, sie gemeinsam mit Gefühl erfassen können. Klassisches Beispiel für solche Prosa-Gedichte hat der französische Dichter Charles Baudelaire (1821-1867,Paris) geliefert. Martin Kari-Gedichte sind jedoch mehr von einem neuzeitlichen Denken bestimmt.

(Englische Übersetzung der Bewertung vom editorial Schreibtisch des FAWQ-Magazines, Caroline Glen).

Paradise, Paul Gauguin

A Glorious Day

Silence still rules over the night. The moon has travelled its path.
It sits at the horizon, waiting to change nightlight into sunny daylight.
The net of little star light holes in the sky have shone
distant messages to resting dark Mother Earth.

A new day is every time born when the fiery sun looks over the
bowed far horizon. First, in a dark blue shimmering haze, adopted
by growing red ribbon-flame walls, then lightening bush, trees and
houses send their long, dark shades on to wider spreading ground.

Vanishing shade-creations accompany silence, stepping back
with time to allow bright orange sunlight to finally flood all the
chosen land with daylight in a piercing yellow disc; this time through
a sky, free of barricading clouds, now an azure-blue spectacle.

Paradies, Paul Gauguin

Ein Herrlicher Tag

Stille herrscht noch in der Nacht.
Der Mond hat seinen Lauf bereits genommen.
Er sitzt am Horizont und wartet, damit die Nacht einen neuen
Tag beginnt. Das Netz der vielen kleinen Sternenlichter am Nachthimmel
hat der ruhenden Mutter Erde leuchtende Boten aus der Ferne gesandt.

Jedes Mal, wenn die Sonne ihre Blicke über den fernen
Horizont wirft, beginnt ein neuer Tag.
Zuerst zögernd in verschleiertem Dunst, dann übergehend in zunehmend
rötlichem Feuer, bringt er Busch, Häuser, Bäume ins Tageslicht und
sendet ihre langen, dunkeln Schatten weiter über Mutters Erde Boden.

Dann begleitet die langsam sich zurückziehenden Schatten noch die Stille
in bereits hellem orangem Sonnenschein, überflutet umliegendes Land
helles Tageslicht mit seiner durchdringenden gelben runden Scheibe;
dieses Mal aus einem Himmel ohne jede Wolkenbank,
in einem völlig klar-blauen Schauspiel.

First, in the air, a cautious birdsong,
then on the ground, life begins a daily routine,
following the rule : the early bird catches the worm.
People, too hear this call, everything seems to move
with them into the awakening morning hours.

Cosy, sunny warmth out of the sky reconciles with a chilly night, eating away foggy mist to prepare a glorious day. More bright sunlight rises into the sky, all creatures rush, rest, vehicles move, people are in buses, trains and further away even our own 'bird-mimics' take into the air.

Silence of the night has gone into hiding, where it is safe
from this daily human hubbub. Nature still holds the key to
recharge our 'batteries' in its forest-oases, wilderness, where
land meets a river or the ocean, mountains, sometimes even
green blossoming city-parks and homey surroundings.

Zuerst verhaltener Vogelgesang aus der Luft,
dann beginnt am Boden der tägliche Lauf
im Sinne : wer zuerst kommt, mahlt zuerst.
Auch Menschen folgen diesem Ruf,
sie werden langsam rastlos, selbst und um sich
in den aufwachenden Stunden des Morgens.

Sanfte Wärme der Sonne versöhnt sich mit der kühleren
Nacht, sie nimmt den verschleiernden Nebel auf, um einen neuen,
herrlichen, klaren Tag vorzubereiten. Die Sonne steigt am Himmel höher,
mehr Menschen eilen, verweilen, Fahrzeuge beeilen die Menschen in Bussen,
wie auch in Zügen, und weiter weg fliehen unsere ‚Vogelversuche' in die Luft.

Dann ist die Stille der Nacht gewichen,
wo sie dem täglichen Treiben entgehen kann.
Noch hält die Natur Oasen der Erholung für uns bereit :
in Wäldern, offener Natur, wo Flüsse im Land ihren Weg
zum Meer suchen, Bergen, selbst im blühenden Grün einer
Stadt, bis in die abgeschirmte Umgebung eines Zuhause.

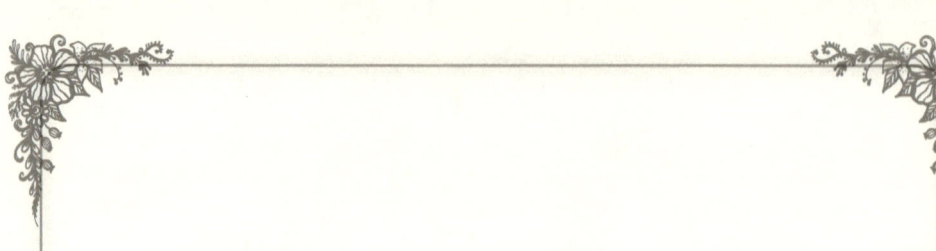

Nature still offers to escape from our hubbub into its oases.
Then a far cry from daily pressures, life can worship a glorious day.
Everything and everybody recognises this from an office,
a workshop, in an open field - the athlete, the sick,
the rich, the poor, the young and the old.

Difficulties then hide in our memories, giving wings to a new,
better hope. Because the sun has taken the reigns of the day, shining
generously, indiscriminately, quietly onto our lucky spot, Mother Earth.
All we see, know, is accidental. The 'glory' of the sun, reconciles us.

Life has never been all sunshine. We grab the sunny moments of life
or go down the road of despair. Day's warmth finally slips into the first
hours after midday, keeping it up for all afternoon. Then the sun hovers
towards the horizon again, resending its longer shadow-creations.

Was wir lieben, nehmen wir gerne mit in die Oasen der Natur.
Tägliche Eile und Forderungen weichen hier, ein herrlicher Tag
nimmt uns dann in seine Arme. Selbst in der Erinnerung lebt ein
Tag so fort, sei es im Bureau, einer Werkstatt, draußen im Freien,
mit dem Sportler, dem Kranken, dem jungen, dem alten Menschen
dem Rastlosen, dem Besinnlichen, dem Armen, dem Reichen.

Schwierigkeiten werden dann leicht vergessen, neue Hoffnung
beflügelt uns. All dies nur deshalb, weil die Sonne den schönen
Tag bringt, zufällig, zuverlässig wechselnd auf Plätzen unserer
geliebten Mutter Erde. Für uns ist und bleibt alles zufällig.
Erkennen wir nicht die Schönheit der Natur im Sonnenlicht,
wird es uns schwer fallen, auch ohne sie den Tage zu ehren.

Das Leben war noch nie nur lauter Sonnenschein.
Sonnige Augenblicke sind da, wahrgenommen zu werden,
denn sonst überkommt uns zu leicht der Kummer.
Die Tageswärme hält zunehmend ihren Zutritt in den Nachmittag,
bis dann die Sonne dem Horizont sich wieder nähert
und erneut ihre langen Schattenbilder uns zeigt.

And so do all daily rush-hours, following into a calmer evening and prepare night-silence to return. The balmy night not hints at the chill yet to come, while the sun's farewell carry cooler hours with a bite in the air, sending us back into houses, where our artificial lights try to replace the sun.

Life still goes on, but slowly is taken over by silence. Daylight creatures worship a rest time, upon which the enlightened stars, the moon face keep equal vigilance over remaining activities and over a sleeping world, to prepare another glorious day. Moon shine and let the sun rest too.

(Words, Martin Kari – 2008)

All unser Leben folgt solchem Wechsel wieder in einen ruhigeren Abend, um die Stille der Nacht vorzubereiten.
Noch verraten die milden Abendstunden nicht die Kühle der Nacht, solange die Sonne nicht Abschied genommen hat.
Viele von uns suchen Zuflucht in Häusern, wo innen künstliches Licht das Tageslicht versucht zu verlängern.

Das Leben geht weiter, jedoch im Schutz von mehr Stille, kommt auch die Tagesarbeit zur Ruhe. Die sinkende Sonne sendet wieder die Sternlichter, den Mond im Himmel, ihre Augen auf unser weiteres Tun, sowie auf die Ruhe, damit ein neuer, herrlicher Tag ihr folgen kann. Lieber Mond, sende uns dein Licht, damit auch die Sonne ruhen kann.

(Worte, Martin Kari, 2008)

Joy of Writing

Leave the daily rush aside,
Sit down and take your mind
On a journey of wishes and worries,
This is the joy of written words.
Thoughts, the first efforts
Towards wishes and worries,
They cross all borders
Like birds in the air.
They can rest on paper,
Or take a journey further,
To meet a few close-people first,
Eventually go out far
To many like-minded people.
But different-minded people , too.
Then time and coincidences
Will catch up with us again,
Feeding back good and less good answers
To our wishes and worries.

(Words, Martin Kari, 2015)

Freude am Schreiben

Fliehe der täglichen Eile,
Setze dich nieder und stimme den Geist
Auf eine Wunsch- und Sorgen- Reise ein,
Dies ist Freude am Schreiben.
Die Gedanken sind frei,
Gegenüber Wünschen sowie Sorgen,
Sie überwinden alle Grenzen,
So wie die Vögel in der Luft.
Sie finden Zuflucht auf Papier,
Oder gehen weiter auf ihrer Reise,
Zuerst zu nahe stehenden Menschen,
Dann aber auch weiter weg,
Zu so manchen Gleichgesinnten,
Anders Gesinnten aber auch.
Jetzt holt uns die Zeit und Zufälligkeit ein,
Gutes sowie weniger Gutes lehren sie uns,
Die Wünsche und Sorgen bleiben,
Der Gewinn ist die Freude.

(Worte, Martin Kari, 2015)

Nature's Cathedral

POETRY PAGES – words: Martin Kari
(FAWQ –Magazine)

The city - concrete jungle - lies a long way back,
Single houses are left behind, too.
A road - beaten track - fields, meadows - all have disappeared.
In a green wall nature's stronghold rises out of its jungle.
Somewhere bush stoops low, allowing passage on foot into obscurity.
Leaves, branches, lianas barricade the interior,
little tree trunks lock-up space, whereas here and there large tree
trunks rise up straight holding a dark roof canopy high into the sky,
leaving little room for sunlight to shine through.
The catbird invisibly mews his penetrating warning,
an intruder has arrived in nature's rainforest cathedral.

A voice, a breaking branch under a foot, all noises are carried
a long way, high up through the canopy,
everything has stopped and is watching from a hiding place.
On the ground, wallabies, possums, tree-kangaroos,
bandicoots, cuscus, brush-turkeys, goannas,
pythons, tree-snakes, lizards and geckos.

Natur Kathedrale

Die Stadt, sein Häusermeer, liegen weit zurück,
selbst einzelne Häuser sind dem Blickfeld entrückt,
die Straße, ein Feldweg, Wiesen und Felder,
alles hat hier geendet. Ein grüner Wall erhebt sich
vor der größten Festung der Natur, dem Urwald.
Niederer Busch läßt nur an einer Stelle in halber
Dunkelheit erkennen: Blätter, Äste, Lianen, sie
versperren den Zugang, Bäume liegen im Weg,
doch streben viel mehr Bäume noch nach oben.
Sie stützen hoch das dunkle Blätterdach
und lassen dem Sonnenlicht nur wenig Raum.
Der Katzenvogel miaut schon seinen Warnruf.

Ein Fremder hat die Natur Kathedrale betreten.
Kein Laut entgeht vom Boden bis in das Dach,
alles wartet gespannt, am Boden: Wallabies,
Possums, Baum Känguruhs, Beuteldachs, Cuscus,
Brush-Turkeys, Goanas, Pythons, Baumschlangen,
Echsen, Geckos. - Halbhoch: Käfer, Schmetterlinge,
Spinnen, Insekten, Zikaden senden in Wellen
ihren Ruf: Der Regen kommt bald. Farben der Papageien leuchten
durch im Grünen Meer, Kingfisher und Sonnenvögel, Schussvögel,

And in mid-area in young treetops: beetles,
butterflies, spiders, and insects.
Cicadas' chirping moves in waves across the forest
cathedral announcing the rain soon to come.
Some of nature's most colourful creatures, king
parrots, rainbow lorikeets, kingfishers, sunbirds,
riflebirds, honeyeaters, regent bowerbirds,
all watch the intruder from high up in the canopy.
All are present in the cathedral, but nothing the
eye initially can meet.

Only when silence has returned,
all creatures large and small start life's daily routines again,
moving, searching, feeding on what the rainforest
holds, sometimes playing, resting, waiting.
Silence of the permanent residents is then broken,
telling each other the different stories with sharp
calls, long songs and noises.
A visitor can observe more near the ground after
the eye has adjusted to dim daylight.
Moist cooler air stores in a constant exchange the

*Honigesser, Regent-Bower-Vögel. All ihnen entgeht
aus dem Dach der Fremde nicht.
Alle halten sie sich in der Kathedrale versteckt,
erst wenn Ruhe zurückkehrt, geht das Leben
weiter mit Suchen, Spielen, Ruhen, Warten. Endlich bricht die Kathedrale ihre eigene Stille, von
überall erheben sich Stimmen, Gesang und Laute,
nicht verständlich für uns Menschen. Der Fremde
nimmt dies wahr zuerst in Bodennähe, sobald das
Auge die Dämmerung durchdringt. Vor allem
herrscht am Boden die Kühle und Nässe, wo
gespeicherter Regen hoffnungsvolles Leben fördert,
ernährt und vorbereitet im Schutz von Büschen,
Bäumen, Blättern, Ästen und Erde.
Hoch oben in den Bäumen warten Blattbecher der Vogel-
Nestfarne gemeinsam mit den Staghorns,
um Licht und Regen schon dort einzufangen.
Noch am Boden ermahnt „wait a while" den eiligen Fremden, „ein wenig zu warten", seinen
Juckreiz zu pflegen. Dann versperren Baumstämme
am Boden dem Fremden den Weg, fordern
ihn auf, den Blick nach oben zu wenden, wie weit
er reicht. So manche Baumsäule beginnt vom
Boden mit mächtigen Wurzeln ihren Lauf nach
oben, den Schwächeren zu umschlingen,
um sich von ihm zu ernähren.*

Rain in the ground feeds hopeful young plant life,
with fallen leaves, branches, and trees.
Bird-nest ferns and stag-horns form leaf-cups high,
up in trees to catch light and moisture.
A wait-a-while creeper makes the hasty visitor wait,
for a while to lick his wounds
from nasty, itchy sting.
Then a massive tree-trunk in the way stops the visitor,
sending his eyes upwards
to look how far he can see.

Some trees spread with flat triangular roots
on the forest floor,
increasing the support of a jungle-giant on the ground.
Huge strangler figs often dominate other tree-giants,
with their massive trunk roots
growing from the top of a host-tree all the way around.
When reaching the ground, the host-tree's fate is sealed,
the fig strangles the host.
Some trunk-roots of the strangler become so huge,
that passages between allow you to walk through.
Old solid lianas also come down from old trees,
often in loops to block a passage.
They never say, "swing on me."

*"Strangler Figs" umwachsen den "Gastgeber-Baum"
von oben nach unten. Erreichen die Wurzeln
den Boden, hat das Schicksal gesprochen, der
Feigenbaum bringt den "Gastgeber" um. Seine
Würgwurzeln stützen sich mächtig am Boden
in einem Labyrinth mit Durchgängen. Doch
nicht alles würgt, was von oben kommt. Auch
Lianen kommen oben vom Blätterdach, stützen
sich in dünnen bis dicken Windungen
zum Boden hin; ihre Schlinge in Bodennähe
heißt noch lange nicht: Schaukel mich, denn
fällt sie herab, weiß der Fremde warum.*

*So teilt sich dem Fremden die Kathedrale mit,
auch im Schutz von gefallenen Bäumen mit
Schimmel, Moos, Ameisen, Schnecken, Schlangen.
Alles folgt dem Kathedralgesetz sich anzupassen.
Keine Ausnahme gilt auch für den Fremden. Das Auge sind die ‚wait a
while', Ameisen, Schlangen, Spinnen. Nur wenige Blumen erfreuen sich
der Dämmerung. Der Schirmbaum nutzt eine Lücke im Wald und lockt
mit seinen leuchtend roten Blütenständen die bunten Lorikeet-Papageien
an. Sie antworten laut, rufen andere, um auch Ablenkung zu schaffen.*

When crushing down from a dwindling height,
only then will we know
how firm, large, and heavy they were,
endangering somebody underneath for sure.

Fungi, mosses, ants, snails
often hide under leaves on the ground.
All life here is told not to make a mistake.
And so the visitor is also bound to do,
when he wants to see something
and stay safe from the rainforest's natural defenses—
wait-a-while, snakes, spiders,
accidentally fallen branches.

Very few flowers develop in this darkness.
Umbrella trees, with their long umbrella-formed leaves,
specially attract lorikeets to their distinct red flower-studs,
creating, with the honey-licking lorikeets,
an incredible colour paradise.

A goanna can rarely be seen,
often in a sunny spot, soaking up the warmth.
When disturbed, they rush in haste up a tree-trunk.
Watching them already reveals
that they sense.

Ein seltener Bewohner ist die „Goanna-Echse".
Wo die Sonne die Kathedrale durchbricht, sieht man sie die
Wärme ruhig aufnehmen. Jeder Störung weicht sie eilig an einem
Baumstamm nach oben aus. Ihre lange, dünne gespaltene
Zunge sucht prüfend die Umgebung vorsichtig im voraus.
Dies ist eine Begegnung mit der Umwelt in der verbliebenen
Natur Kathedrale. Auch für viele Bäume ist sie
unveränderlich Heimat geblieben. Selbst wenn nur in
Oasen, die Natur Kathedrale lebt noch in Australien.

Die ältesten Natur Kathedralen sind in Australien.
Trotz ihrer geringen Größe, beherbergen sie noch
die größte Vielfalt an Leben in einem Platz. Alte
erfahrene Baumriesen wie : Black Apple, Rote Zeder,
Bunya Pine, sind seine Bewohner seit Urzeiten.
Farnbäume senden ihr frisches Grün nahe dem Boden
in den vorherrschenden dunkelbraunen bis
dunkelgrünen Tönen dieser Schattenschutz-Welt.
In diesem Schutz beginnen bescheiden Flüsse ihren
Lauf. Wo Licht und Wasser einen Platz finden,
siedeln sich auch gerne Palmen an. Wasser beginnt
seine Reise durchs Land von hier.

Their direct environment, with constant searching,
a thin long tongue—
an encounter with ancient prehistory.
In nature's cathedral, many trees establish
an existence over a long period of time,
and can therefore often be found today
only in one place.
Rainforests in Australia are the oldest on earth,
harbouring the richest variety in living forms,
despite the small remaining forest pockets.
Black apple, red cedar, bunya pine—
trees still growing after hundreds of years
into rainforest giants.
Tree ferns usually come up in penetrating light-corridors,
giving the lower forest area a fine green shine
against the mostly dark-brown
and dark-green forest shades.
Lower areas of a rainforest can harbour a watercourse.
Palms near a water-flow
add a tropical image to the forest.

Water usually leaves a forest,
starting a journey through countryside,
mostly without the protection of the forest.
Only a constant supply from the forest
gives a river its strength.

*Diese Reise steht jedoch im Schutz der Kathedrale,
wie weit Wasser seinen Lauf nehmen kann. Ohne
den Schutz verliert sich das Wasser im Land. Zeit
hat keinen Zugang in die Kathedrale gefunden,
Vögel verkünden pünktlich aus dem Blattgewölbe,
schon seit eh und jeh, den Tag und Nacht-Beginn. Viele Kathedral-
Bewohner erwachen erst in der kühleren Nacht ; dies sind :
Possums, Bandicoots, Geckos und Fledermäuse. Wer am Tag den
Schutz der Kathedrale verläßt, kehrt mit der Hitze vom Land
zurück. Sein schützendes Dach tragen die erfahrend-sten
Bäume, sie schaffen auch die notwendige Ruhe.*

*Der Besuch in der Natur Kathedrale läßt den
ahnen, wo Ruhe und neue Kräfte verweilen.
Zu erhalten, was noch verblieben, ist eine Pflicht,
dringend so wie auch vornehm, damit auch nachkommende Generationen
dieses Paradies auf Erden noch erleben können. Verlassen wir heute die
Kathedrale der Natur, bleibt ihr Grünes Bollwerk unverändert zurück.
Felder, Wiesen, Feldwege, Straßen bringen uns wieder näher dem
Häusermeer. Und schließlich in unsere eigene
Schöpfung einer Kathedrale, fern vom Schutz
des Urwaldes, in die Stadt mit ihrem Dschungel.*

(Worte, Martin Kari – 2009)

the start for its journey.
Without it, a river ceases to exist.
Time in a rainforest cathedral seems to stop.
Birds from the high canopy tell with their voices
when morning and nightfall arrive.
In the night's darkness many rainforest residents
waken to life, possums, geckos, bandicoots, bats,
seeking the cooler hours.
To leave the rainforest cathedral during the day is
to bring back the open heat of the land.

The rainforest is a cathedral, a quiet place, where
high trees support its roof, creating a huge dome
under which life finds protection.
Visiting a rainforest cathedral gives us back nature's
very basic strength for our body and mind.
We have an obligation to preserve what is left of
the rainforest,
So that future generations can also experience this
paradise on earth.
When leaving the rainforest cathedral the green wall
of nature's jungle remains behind unchanged.
Meadows, fields, beaten tracks, roads bring us closer
to single houses again and finally back to our own
jungle creation.
The city concrete jungle.

FAWQ – Gedichts – Worte

Von der Feder des Gedicht Editors: Caroline Glen
Mai 2009, Brisbane-Australien

„Dieses Gedicht von Martin Kari ist ein Prosa-Gedicht, eine Verbindung von Prosa und einem Gedicht. Es ist kein ‚freier Text', sondern ein mehr zusammenhängender Text. Prosa-Gedichte kommen direkt vom Herzen. Sie sind nicht bestimmt ausschließlich von einem Format oder Zeilen-Gestaltung. Es geht um die Wahrheit. Die Länge kann sehr unterschiedlich sein und lehnt sich an Geschichts-Erzählung an. Seine Schwerpunkte beruhen nicht auf Intel-lekt, welcher unaufhörlich auf der Suche nach Neuland ist, an Spaß jedoch zu leicht vorbei-schießt. Seine Sprache ist direkt, ohne Umschweife. Der Dichter bringt ein starkes Bedürfnis zum Ausdruck, mit dem Leser zu tei-len, was er sieht und empfindet. Dieses Prosa- Gedicht liest sich leicht, der Leser begegnet kei-nen Hemmschuhen. Die Aussagen sind unmißverständlich.

FROM THE POETRY EDITOR'S DESK

This poem by Martin Kari is a prose poem, which is a combination of prose and poetry. It is not 'free verse' which is a more contracted form. Prose poetry generally is written very much from the heart. It does not concern itself too much with form and line ending. It aims at telling the truth. It has variable lengths and is often written in story style. It does not try to be very clever, constantly inviting stress to find fresh metaphor, simile. It generally tells what it wants to in plain language. The poet expresses a strong desire to share with the reader what he sees, how he feels. The prose poem is comfortable in its telling, not having to rely on the hammered 'show don't tell.' We get a clear message.

Readers of this poem will experience with the poet his joy in his observations of what nature is showing/ providing for him. We cannot help but enter the rainforest with him and be rewarded.

Baudelaire was renowned for his prose poems.

       Caroline Glen – May 2009 – FAWQ Scope Magazine.

Leser dieses Gedichtes teilen die Freude, welche der Dichter erfährt mit seinen Beobachtungen, direkt in einem Austausch mit Mutter Natur, der wir alle unser Dasein verdanken. Wir kommen nicht umhin, der Einladung des Dichters in den Urwald zu folgen und wir werden nicht enttäuscht. Martin Kari folgt mit seinem Gedicht in den Fußspuren des französischen Dichters Baudelaire, welcher von 1821 bis 1867 haupt-sächlich in Paris lebte. Martin gibt unserer Zeit wertvolle neue Impulse.

(Übersetzt aus der original englischen Beurteilung der ältesten Schriftsteller Vereinigung Australiens, welcher Martin Kari als ein Mitglied zugehört.)

Dreams & Reality

Sometimes dreams can come true,
Alike dreams in a cloud,
High above reality's ground.
A look from such distance
Makes everything to appear smaller,
Keeping Good from Bad apart.
Our dreams then take new steps,
Further than reality would allow,
Imagination keeps us caught,
Be it with hope,worries, joy,but also fear,
These moments of life receive renewal
Through our most secret dreams,
Open eventually even a window
Into the eternal dream after life.
But when dreams again escape,
Life repeated has us in a firm grip,
Truly challenging our dreams
In a world marked mainly with reality.

(Words, Martin Kari-2012)

Traum & Wirklichkeit

Manchmal werden Wünsche wahr,
Gleich einem Traum in einer Wolke,
Hoch über dem Boden der Wirklichkeit.
Ein Blick dann mit solchem Abstand,
Lässt alles nur kleiner erscheinen
Und trennt das Gute vom Bösen.
Unsere Träume nehmen neue Schritte,
Weiter als die Wirklichkeit dies erlauben würde.
Unsere Vorstellung nimmt uns im Traum gefangen,
In Hoffnung, Sorge, Freude, aber auch in Angst.
Augenblicke des Lebens erfahren Verlängerungen
In unseren geheimsten Träumen,
Öffnen vielleicht sogar ein Fenster
In den ewigen Traum nach dem Leben.
Wenn Träume dann aber wieder fliehen,
Hat uns das Leben erneut in festem Griff
Und fordert unsere Träume wahrhaftig heraus
In einer von Wirklichkeit geprägten Welt.

(Worte, Martin Kari-2012)

Fire

Fire is final, yes and no! It burns down everything,
but it can create new growth in its aftermath.
This contrast of destruction and bringer of life is the life
cycle of nature. As such it must be regarded as controversial.
Where do we find the source of this controversy?
We are standing right on it, on our fireball of Earth.
Australia in particular, in its isolation from the rest of
the world, displays the evolution of fire survival and the
challenges of fire versus the creation of new life.
It is also said nothing is totally bad even after
fire, as long as hope survives.

(Words, Martin Kari – 2014)

Feuer

Feuer ist endgültig, ja und nein ! Es vernichtet alles,
zugleich fördert es aber auch neues Wachstum,
sowie neue Anstrengungen im Nachherein.
Solche Gegensätzlichkeit müssen wir Menschen in einem
Ablauf der Natur hinnehmen, weil alles in der
Natur nur in Gegensätzlichkeiten besteht.
Wo ist im Falle Feuer die hauptsächliche
Gegensätzlichkeit zu suchen ?
Stehen wir mit unseren Füßen nicht auf ihm,
unserem Feuer-Ball Erde ?
Von hier nimmt alles seinen Lauf.
Insbesondere ist es Australien,
welches in seiner vom Rest der Welt abgeschirmten
Entwicklung mit uralt bewährten
Überlebens Praktiken seiner Natur durch Feuer
neues Leben bis heute weiß zu schaffen.
Auch Feuer trifft das Natur Gesetz der
Aufrechterhaltung von Polaritäten:
Mit Feuer ist nicht nur alles schlecht geworden,
solange Hoffnung nicht auch noch verloren gegangen ist.

(Worte, Martin Kari 2014)

Outback Journey in Australia

Time must have stopped, life has fallen silent,
a far cry away from every day's life in a city.
The sun reigns all year, the views are wide and open.
The eye can search, we are in the Outback.

A day starts here like every other one, sunlight opens the sky in a colourful dis-play, from dark-orange direct above the bowed horizon, to orange, red, yellow, the higher this fire-ball climbs. Shades born by individual bush out of the dark, shorten, until daylight makes them disappear.

Birds, single, small, large, in flocks – White, black, pink, rich in striking colours. Cockatoos, Magpies, Ravens, Galahs, Finches, Lorikeets, the occasional Wedge-tail Eagle,

Reise Ins Outback

1

Die Zeit muß hier stehen geblieben sein, alles Leben hat sich in Schweigen gehüllt, weit weg vom rastlosen Treiben der Stadt. Hier regiert die Sonne das ganze Jahr, die Sicht erreicht überall den Horizont, unsere Augen können suchen, wir sind im Outback von Australien.

2

Jeder Tag nimmt hier seinen gleichen Lauf, Die Sonne eröffnet am Himmel ihr farbiges Spiel, in tiefem Orange über dem gewölbten Horizont, dann wechselt der aufsteigende Feuerball seine Farben zu hellem Orange, Rot und Gelb. Schatten einzelner hartnäckiger Büsche treten aus dem Dunkel zunehmend kürzer hervor, bis helles Tageslicht sie verdrängt.

3

Vögel, alleine, in Gesellschaft mit anderen, kleine sowie große, weiß, schwarz, rosa, in auffallenden bunten Farben : Kakadus, Magpies, Raben, Galahs, Finken, Lorikeets, gelegentlich der Wedge-Tailed Adler, sie alle steigen mit lauten Stimmen in den

they all fly into the sky of a new-born day, not without announcing it very sharp and loud. To whom the birds make their announcement? Nobody is here to listen ! Have they got the window to our creator?

The sun rises in a crystal blue sky, sending heat-waves towards Mother Earth, on the increase, large red-kangaroos, small wallabies, emus, wombats, brumbies, cattle, wild pigs only occasionally, they all move into hiding in the vast bush, looking for the protection from the heat of the day.

In a contrast, the large family of snakes and lizards search for the early sun of the day, feeding off the heat waves. Few people only move after a business in the early hours of a day. Not long will it take that Mother Earth sends back the heat, it cannot take more in the middle of the day, shifting then the air and creating distorted pictures of the Outback, everything turns silent.

Himmel eines neuen Tages ; wem gilt der Ruf ? Wo ist jemand, der den Ruf wahrnimmt ? Begrüßen sie den Schöpfer von uns allen ?

4

Die Sonne nimmt den Lauf im klaren, blauen Himmelszelt und sendet Wärme auf die Erde, endlich eilen große, rote Känguruhs, kleine Wallabies, Emus, Wombats, Wildpferde, Rinder, manchmal auch Wildschweine, dem Schatten noch vor der Tageshitze nachzugehen. Tageshitze sucht jedoch Vieles was kriecht auf, Schlangen und Echsen weichen ihr nicht aus. Morgenstunden sind nur für den Wachsamen, denn bald sendet die Erde die Hitze wieder zurück.

5

Mitte des Tages herrscht dann, hitzegesättigt übernimmt die Luft ihr Spiel mit Bildern, während alles wieder Ruhe sucht. Vom hohen Himmel blickt die Sonne auf alles unter ihr. Autos ,ob auf fester oder Staubstraße,fahren besser, um der Hitze zu wehren. Anhalten gibt der Sonne Zeit Hitze aufzubauen. Hilfe muß im Outback nicht geschrieben werden, wer leben will, muß hier auch helfen. Nach Stunden unterwegs , verkündet die Hand bei einer Begegnung, „alles ist gut".

From its highest point in the sky the sun has penetrated everything. Travelling in a car on a road, with or without dust, makes you then best moving. A breeze through a car can keep minds alive. Stopping with a car in summer, the sun will hit you hard. The law of the Outback is support and help. It is nowhere written down, it is a must for a living, travelling, surviving here.

With long hours on the road another car appears, hand signs speak for everything being o.k. Stopping generally indicates a problem ; in a changing world, caution is also here not out of place. Changes from outside take a foothold only slowly in the Outback. Heat, drought, floods, winds, a resisting nature, successfully have put on the brakes on our development needs, so far.

6

Anhalten hingegen spricht oft für Probleme. Doch bleibt guter Rat selten auf der Strecke, Vorsicht gegenüber dem Unbekannten zu üben. Vorsicht ist zwar die Mutter aller Weisheiten, im Outback ist ihr Feind zum Glück noch fern. Dafür sind es Hitze, Trockenheit, Flut, Stürme, die unbeugsame Natur, welche immer noch Entwicklungen erfolgreich bremsen. Schon weit im Westen von der Pazifik Küste wartet die Grenze von Queensland. Weite Weizenfelder warten einsam auf Ernte, Häuser sind schon lange gewichen.

7

Busch und Steppe wechseln sich ab, wo die Steppe wachsen durfte, steht Gras mannshoch und passt sich dem Gelb der Weizenfelder an. Känguruhs, Emus, Rinder sind hier zu Hause. Der Reisende muß ein gutes Auge für sie haben und auch noch auf die eiligen Riesen-Lastwagen. Road Trains fahren geschäftig weit und schnell, Anhalten ist nicht ihre Aufgabe, Staub in der Luft nimmt vor allem den anderen die Sicht. Drei bis vier doppel-stöckige Anhänger fahren oft Rinder. Ihr Fahrtwind und Sog fordern Respekt auf Straßen, anhalten ausweichen ist die beste Antwort in einer Begegnung mit ihnen.

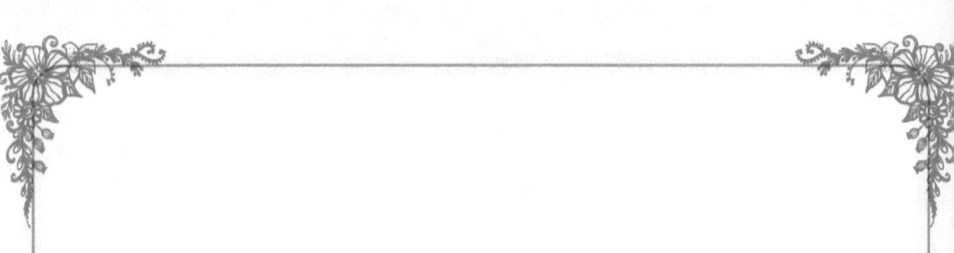

2000 kilometres distance from the tropical coast of East-Australia, the border of Queensland and the Northern Territory is not far. Vast rolling fields of wheat around Longreach are just behind us, the green bush has claimed back its territory for awhile, only grassland, high standing after a wet season, yellow when mature.

On the road are also the road trains, moving goods, life-stock, harvests in long truck-chains. They are the king of the Outback roads, demanding the right of a lane, up to 5 long trailers can make up a road-train. They move very fast, have long distances to go and won't stop. Sidewise moving trailers ask oncoming traffic better to stop, on the side of the road. The driver of a road-train cannot see, what happens in a dust-cloud behind. Massive bull-bars on the front of road-trains keep everything off the road: kangaroos, cattle, better not another car.

8

*Road Trains schützen sich selbst mit „Bull-Bars",
Alles in ihrem Weg, schieben sie schnell von der Straße ; Känguruhs,
Rinder, besser keine Autos. In der Nacht gilt, weg von der Straße
bleiben, Tiere suchen die Nachtkühle auf für Futtersuche, wenn die
Hitze des Tages gewichen ist. Sowohl am Tag, als in der Nacht bleibt
vieles dem Auge verborgen. Menschen stören die natürliche Ordnung.
Wir gefährden nur uns und die Tiere in ihren Gewohnheiten.*

9

*Zum Ende des Tages hört die Sonne langsam auf ihre Wärme weiter
auszusenden. Die Nacht jedoch schafft es nicht immer, Kühle zuzulassen.
Schatten werden wieder länger, bis die Nacht Einzug gehalten hat, denn
erst am nächsten Morgen gewinnt Kühle ihren Einzug für wenigstens ein
paar Stunden, bevor ein neuer Tag den Sonnen-Kreislauf wieder aufnimmt.*

10

*Ein „Caravan Park" nahe einer Siedlung bietet
eine gute Möglichkeit für eine Bleibe
während der Nacht. An seinem Eingang wartet
für den neuen Besucher die Aufschrift
auf einem Karton an der Türe : „Besitzer ist
ausgeflogen, die acht Dollar Gebühren werfe*

At night it can be only recommended to stay off the road. The animals hiding during the heat of the day are moving and feeding then. Surprisingly much life is waking up during an Outback night. Human presence is disturbing it, animals flee from us, putting them and us in danger on the road.

Towards the end of a day the heat starts losing power, heat remains however well into the night. Shades become longer until darkness of the night takes over. Only in the early morning hours does cooler air move across the Outback.

A caravan-park near a hamlet is a welcome stop for a night. At the shed of the entrance is visibly attached :"Owner is out, leave your fees of $8 in the mailbox, thanks." City-folk, foreigners, Interstate-travellers are found here of a sudden, but hardly any locals.

in den Briefkasten, Danke schön !" Städter, Ausländer, reisende Australier trifft man hier an, aber keine Ansässigen aus der Gegend. Hier erfährt man, daß ein Jeder dem Outback in seiner Art und Weise gegenüber tritt. Auch deshalb unterscheiden sich die Geschichten der „Caravan-Park"- Bewohner wie die Leute selbst untereinander.

11

Die Ansässigen teilen die Geschichten nicht, sie wissen Bescheid. Auch in der Nacht ist die Straße nie weit, die Stille bricht gelegentlich der Donner vieler eiliger Reifen eines „Road Trains", welcher auch in der Nacht nicht zur Ruhe kommt. Sonst herrscht völlige Stille der Nacht, unter dem Himmels-Gewölbe mit seinen glitzernden, neugierigen Sternen.

12

Die ersten Stunden der Nacht sitzen die Reisenden hier und da zusammen um ein kleines Feuer. Geschichten helfen die Zeit vergehen lassen, bis endlich die Hitze des Tages sich verabschiedet. Dann hat auch die Stille der Nacht den Park erfasst : Grillen zirpen aus ihren Verstecken, von nah und fern. Ihre Kunde fliegt in Wellen durch die verharrende Luft der Nacht. Schatten zwischen den Eukalypten und Akazien

Everybody experiences the Outback his way. Therefore people and their stories in caravan-parks differ like the people themselves. Locals have less stories to tell, because they know. The nearby road delivers during the night only the occasional thunder-like passage of a road-train. The dark night is otherwise immersed into silence under the roof of a glittering sky.

People in the caravan-park sit together around a small fireplace, exchanging their stories and waiting long into the night before the heat of the day gives way to a cooler night. Crickets rub their wings out of their hiding, sending messages in waves through the air of this night. A sudden fast moving shade between the few Eucalypt and Acacia-trees make up this caravan-park in the endless grass and bushland surrounding it.

There are also the curious bats ; sometimes even kangaroos come out of the bush very close to the people, making their inspections on what is happening in their territory. Another morning does not fail to announce a new day. The far horizon sends again the first cautious light into the black uprising sky-dome.

verschwinden in der Dunkelheit so schnell, wie sie zu
dem kleinen Platz gekommen sind, aus der umliegenden
Mehrheit von Busch, Steppe und weiten Feldern.

13
Neugierige Fledermäuse melden auch ihren Besuch an; Känguruhs
wagen sich in die Nähe, um heraus-zufinden, was hier in der
Nacht auf ihrem Gebiet noch so vor sich geht. Die Nacht weicht
wieder ohne zu fehlen und räumt einem neuen Tag seine Rolle
wieder ein. Am Horizont erscheinen die ersten vorsichtigen Farben-
Spiele in dem dunkeln Dom der Nacht, über uns Allen.

14
Auch für uns ist dies der Startschuß für einen neuen Tag, obwohl
die anderen Geschichts-Erzähler des Vorabends der Schlaf gründlich
überkommen hat. Alles findet bei uns seinen Platz wieder im
Auto, aus Rücksicht lassen wir den Motor nur kurz sich
einlaufen und schon sind wir wieder unterwegs im Outback-Australien.

This is the moment , our new day starts. Everything is packed away into the car in its own place. We allow the engine to run warm only for a moment, not to disturb other people in their sleep. Shortly after we are back on the road, alone, lights of the car show us the way. A pair of close red points in the light beams announce a kangaroo on the side of the road, where the only green grass is at the bitumen-border. Speed is immediately reduced to watch the kangaroo anxiously waiting in the dark. Will it keep feeding or jump ? "Roo" is a master in sudden movements. Strong back legs give them the power to jump a few metres out of the bush on to the road right in front of a car. The red colour of our car made the "roo" to stay, reminding it eventually of blood, when hit by a car.

The morning spectacle is repeated once again, daylight consumes the dark in a colourful display. Two and a half hours have pioneered us into a new day, before the first car passed us. A sign of a homestead attracts our attention on the side of the road. We stop, move off the road, despite hardly any traffic.

(Words, Martin Kari – 2012)

15

Zuerst zeigen die Scheinwerfer noch den Weg für das Auto. Rötliche zwei Punkte am Rande der Straße sind die Augen eines gestörten Känguruhs bei der Suche nach dem wenigen grünen Gras am Rande der Straße. Der Fuß geht schnell vom Gas, die Augen des aufmerksamen Fahrers beobachten jetzt : Wird das Känguruh weiter fressen, oder springen? Seine starken Hinterläufe befähigen das Känguruh aus dem Busch seitlich der Straße in überraschend weiten Sprüngen auf dem Fluchtweg auch mitten auf der Straße, direkt vor einem Auto unerwartet zwischenzulanden. Hat die rote Farbe unseres Autos abgeschreckt, weil Känguruhs bereits erfahren hatten, was passiert, wenn sie auf der Straße im falschen Augenblick landen ?

16

Das Schauspiel des erwachenden Tages wiederholt sich am Nachthimmel. Licht bannt erst langsam, dann aber entschlossen die Dunkelheit in seinem gewohnten farbigen Spiel. Zwei und einhalb Stunden hat uns der neue Tag auf den Weg gerufen, bevor ein anderes Fahrzeug uns wieder begegnet.
Ein Schild an der Seite der Straße
lenkt unsere Aufmerksamkeit zu ihm.
Obwohl kein Auto weit und breit,
halten wir an der Stelle der Straße an.

(Worte, Martin Kari-2012)

The Wheel Barrow

Let's give a voice to the wheel barrow, too,
with a limit of 100 words only.

The wheel on its own cannot do much
And so cannot the barrow.
To be true to its origin, the barrow needs
A bear behind it to make a wheel working.
And the ones using the wheel barrow
Know only too well what wonderful tool
It can be around a house,
In a garden, building a house.
It takes and moves everything
That fits into its barrow :
Leaves, branches, soil, sand, stones, cement,
Mortar, bricks, timber, tiles
And even joins the fun
To eventually wheel a child
In lieu of a pram
Which all depends
On the person's bear-skills.

(Words, Martin Kari, 2015)

Der Schubkarren

Was ein Schubkarren mit nur 100 Worten zu sagen hat:

*Alleine kann auch ich, das Rad vom Schubkarren, Nicht
viel ausrichten; genau so aber auch meine Karre.
Meiner Existenz gerecht zu werden, brauche ich noch
Jemanden, der mich anhebt und mein Rad bewegt.
Und wer hinter mir steht, weiß allzu gut,
Was für ein gutes Werkzeug ich bin. Um ein Haus herum bin ich nützlich :
Was mir passt, nehme ich ohne Murren auf :
Blätter, Äste, Erde, Sand, Steine, Zement,
Gips, Ziegeln, Holz, Platten,
Sogar Spaß kann ich haben,
Wenn ein Kind statt mit dem Kinderwagen,
Mit mir und meinem Rad einen Ausflug,
Um ein Haus herum mit richtiger Führung macht.*

(Worte, Martin Kari 2015)

Love is Not Only a Word

Love is a peculiar game , too,
It goes from person to person,
Its ball is played with unwritten rules,
Catching up only with the open player.
However not with its great variety,
Because limits apply also here,
To follow rules for the single and all.
Sometimes a coincident can help,
Another time it is poor luck or intention,
And when hope leads this game,
All doors and gates are open for possibilities,
Be it committed, pronounced or not,
Nevertheless love too lives in the present,
The past, up to a hopeful future,
Where life is not hanging by a thread,
Still going through the ups and downs of life,
Granting strength with, without possessions
Even when put to the real test,
Love lasts in the end longer
Than anything else in life,
Until we finally depart this world.
Love lives with us,
Only it can survive us,
There, where its diverse thread
With sympathy, consideration, devotion
Allow life to move on.

(Words, Martin Kari-2016)

Die Liebe ist Nicht nur ein Wort ..

Sondern der best heilende Gedanke

Die Liebe ist ein seltsames Spiel,
Sie wandert von Einem zum Anderen.
Ihr Ball spielt nach eigenen Regeln,
Erfasst nur den, der weiß mitzuspielen.
Jedoch noch lange nicht in seiner Vielfalt,
Denn Einschränkung fordert auch hier,
Spielregeln zu folgen für jeden und alle.
Einmal tritt Zufall hinzu,
Ein ander Mal Glück, oder Absicht,
Und wenn Hoffnung das Spiel führt,
Stehen allen Möglichkeiten Türen und Tore offen,
Selbst bewußt, erkennbar, oder auch nicht,
Denn auch Liebe lebt in der Gegenwart,
Der Vergangenheit, bis hin zu einer Zukunft.
Nur muß sein Faden aufrecht verbleiben,
Durch des Lebens Höhen und Tiefen,
mit und ohne Besitz Festigkeit gewähren,
Auch wenn Zerreißproben ihn fordern.
Am Ende dauert Liebe länger,
Als alles andere im Leben,
Bis hin zum endlichen Scheiden.
Die Liebe lebt mit uns,
Nur Sie lebt nach uns weiter,
Dort, wo sein vielfältiger Faden
Mit Verständnis, Rücksicht, Hingabe,
Ein Weiterleben ermöglicht hat.

(Worte, Martin Kari, 2016)
(Erschienen auch in „Die besten Gedichte der Neuzeit", 2016)

Falling Leaves - Autumn

Winds are blowing, leaves are going,
From close and far they whisper,
The eternal melody of changes.

Spring finally brings again a start,
Into new life during all mighty summer,
First with tender buds.

But then opening into nature's roof,
Primarily green and dense,
To give shelter and shade during summer.

Gentle breezes, fine perfumes,
Life's veins of water and warmth,
They all escort new life into the next change.

Snatching into the beauty of autumn,
Leaves decorate now colours,
To a farewell or a show.

But who should benefit from it ?
The leaves still whisper the melody of change,
What has been created, is passed on.

Fallende Blätter - Herbst

Winde wehen, Blätter gehen,
Aus nah und ferner flüstern sie
Das Lied des Wandels ohn' Unterlass.

Frühjahr eröffnet wieder seinen Reigen,
Mit neuem Leben in allen Zweigen,
Erst wenig sichtbar in vielen Knospen.

Dann aber entfaltet die Wärme der Sonne,
Das hoffnungserfüllte Dach der Natur,
Mit vielen anderen Blättern,

Vornehmlich grün und dicht,
Als Schutz und Schatten,
In einem neuen, nahen Sommer.

Laue Lüfte, feine Düfte,
Begleiten Lebensadern wie Wasser und Wärme,
In seinen neuen Wandel.

Aufraffen in die neue Schönheit Herbst,
Blätter schmücken jetzt die Farben,
Zum Abschied oder einer Schau.

Again the hopeful little buds,
They come to life,
And the Old must give way to the New.

The old leaves finally leave the branches,
In a last charisma of a beauty,
They sail supported with wind to the ground.

Only to pause in a carpet,
Once more colourful,
Until fate of change has caught up with them.

Sometimes feet, hurried wheels on the ground,
Assist the change of the leaves,
Into a colourless new look.

Mother Earth has brought to life leaves , too,
And there is no escape,
From returning to Mother Earth less charismatic.

(Words, Martin Kari, "Brentano Lyric Award" 2016)

Nur wem soll dies alles gelten?
Noch flüstern Blätter das Lied des Wandels,
Was geschaffen, wird weiter gegeben,

Wieder in hoffnungsvollen kleinen Knospen,
Um den Kreislauf des Wandels neu zu beleben,
Muß Alt dem Neuen weichen.

Blätter verlassen nun die Zweige,
Im letzten Aufbegehren farbiger Schönheit,
Segeln sie mit Hilfe des Windes zum Boden.

Nur um dort in einem Teppich,
Farbenfroh noch einmal zu verharren,
Bis dann das Schicksal des Wandels sie einholt.

Manchmal sind es Füße, eilige Räder,
Welche dem Wandel der Blätter helfen
In ein farbloses Gewandt.

Auch Blätter kommen von der Erde
Und fallen weniger selbstbewußt
Zurück zur Mutter Erde.

———•⊰⊱•———

(Worte, Martin Kari, 2015)
(BRENTANO GEDICHT UND GESELLSCHAFTS PREIS 2016)

Winter (English)

Winter winds blow again cold,
One time less, another time more,
Depending much on chances.

Does it know where to go ?
Quiet rules above all,
Allowing New to be re-born.

Mainly dry, cold, snow, storm,
Take their turns in an exchange,
Protected, hidden, much is waiting.

Who could possibly benefit from it ?
Or, why has it to be like this ?
Can words find the answer ?

What has already long lasted,
Doesn't need words to explain,
Everything wants to repeat itself.

Even in opposition to warmth,
Winter leaves his window open,
For beauty to stay on board.

Winter (deutsch)

Winter Winde blasen wieder kalt,
Einmal weniger, einmal mehr,
Je nach Lust und neuer Liebe.

Weiß er, wohin es geht?
Seine Ruhe regiert über Allem,
Um Neues wieder zu gestalten.

Trockenheit, Kälte, Schnee, Sturm,
Sie lösen sich ab im Wechsel,
Geschützt, versteckt wartet Alles.

Wem soll das wohl alles dienen?
Oder, warum muß das so sein?
Finden Worte die Antwort?

Was schon lange hat gewährt,
Bedarf keiner Worte mehr.
Alles will sich noch wiederholen.

Selbst in Anfechtung der Wärme,
Läßt Winter sein Fenster offen,
Um Schönheit nicht zu verlieren.

Much however goes into hiding,
What warmth has revealed,
To seek protection in life that battles on.

Warmth becomes wishful thinking,
Animals wish their way in hiding,
And plants await change for the better.

White magnificence rules the rain,
While the cold brings silence, too,
And everything learns the waiting game.

Winter also loses with time,
Its thorn of severity,
So warmth comes out of hiding again.

First gradually, not always noticeably,
But time lends always a helping hand,
To make happen small and fine.

When such beginning succeeds,
Many doors are open again.
To welcome a new springtime.

(Worte, Martin Kari, 2017)

Trotzdem versteckt Vieles sich,
Was Wärme offenbart hat,
Schutzsuchend im Weiterleben.

Menschen fronen der Wärme,
Tiere im Versteck,
Und Pflanzen im Wandel.

Weisse Pracht statt Regen,
Kälte bringt auch Schweigen,
Alles lernt erneut das Warten.

Doch auch Winter verliert,
Den ‚Stachel' seiner Härte,
Und Wärme kommt aus dem Versteck.

Erst langsam, nicht immer spürbar,
Doch Zeit weiß wieder zu helfen,
Sichtbar, zuerst klein aber fein.

Ist solcher Anfang gelungen,
Sind Türen und Tore geöffnet,
Für die Neue Zeit, Frühjahr.

(Worte, Martin Kari, 2017)

Springtime

Spring bells are ringing again
Bringing back the mildness of sunny days
They flatter us in many wholesome ways.

New life remains first hidden,
In many forms alike,
Emerging with single voices first.

Grass with its new green,
Bush shows tender buddings,
Trees prepare their leafy green.

New growth aims higher up,
Who is behind this new awakening ?
Not us, is it nature, our creator ?

And when emerging visibly,
No draught, not even fire,
Can stop this battle of nature .

What is this battle good for ?
To continue what has been left ,
From nature's previous answers.

No new life without a battle,
Whether we like it or not,

Frühling

Neue Winde wehen,
Laue Lüfte gehen,
Aus Fern und Nah verkünden sie:

Der Frühling ist da,
Erst zögernd verhalten,
Dann aber mit aller Macht.

Gras findet wieder sein Neues Grün,
Büsche sprießen mit kleinen Knospen,
Auch Bäume schlagen aus mit ihrem Grün.

Neues Wachstum will höher hinaus,
Wer ist wohl hinter solchem Erwachen?
Nicht wir, sondern Natur, unser Schöpfer.

Und wenn all dies wird sichtbar,
Keine Trockenheit, selbst Feuer,
Vermag solcher Behauptung Einhalt bieten.

Aber wozu ist dies wiederum gut?
Etwas fortzusetzen, wo Natur
Mit Ihrem Sagen hatte gewartet.

Hoffnung neu auszusprechen,
Daß Altes dem Neuen weichen muß,
Denn so ist der Lauf des Lebens.

Sun and rain let grow grass,
Make explode the buddings of bush,
Trees send leafy shade to protect new life.

An orchestra like, with its symphony,
It sends all good around,
In a selection for a survival.

What flies, spans its wings anew,
Animals form new family bonding,
Even humans come closer again.

And when all this is at its best,
The carpet is readily laid out,
To welcome a mighty summer.

(Words – Martin Kari – Sept. 2017)

Endlich wächst selbst das Gras,
Sonne und Regen eröffnen den Blüten-Segen, Baum-
Dächer spenden schützend Schatten.

Einem Orchester gleich mit seiner Symphonie,
Erklingen weit und breit seine Töne,
In Harmonie für ein Weiterleben.

Wer fliegen kann, übt erneut seine Flügel,
Bodenständig widmet man sich der Familie,
Selbst Menschen rücken näher zusammen.

Und wenn all dies ist gut unterwegs,
Dann liegt auch der Rote Teppich bereit,
Den allmächtigen Sommer zu empfangen.

(Worte, Martin Kari – Sept. 2017)

Summer

When Spring at its height,
Then Summer takes over,
All the 'New' from Spring is tested.

The sun is rising higher,
Extending also daylight hours,
To help life receive sunny sides, too.

It spoils places selectively,
Either enough, too little or too much,
And rain follows a same selection.

Life which was hiding,
Openly comes out,
To join summer in its symphony.

Who can hear these melodies,
Is preparing for more growth,
While young life receives its chances.

Plants, animals, we humans,
Compete in strength and beauty,
For better days to come or not, too.

Sommer

Wenn Frühjahr sein Lob verdient hat,
Dann hält Sommer seinen Eintritt,
Und alles Neue muß sich bewähren.

Die Sonne steigt höher am Himmel,
Sie gibt den Tagen mehr Licht,
Hilft Leben mit ihren sonnigen Seiten.

Auch Sommer hat Lieblingsplätze,
Schenkt genug, zu wenig oder zu viel,
Und Regen folgt denselben Spuren.

Leben welches versteckt war,
Kommt jetzt offen heraus,
Mitzuwirken im Sommer Konzert.

Wer ein Ohr für solche Stimmen hat,
Hilft Neuem Wachstum,
Alles erlebt neue Zufälle.

Pflanzen, Tiere, Menschen,
Messen sich in Stärke und Schönheit,
Alles wünscht sich bessere Tage.

Humans like to worship the sun,
Less with work under a shade,
Which likewise pleases the sun.

Rain rushes into rivers,
In a call from nature,
To also worship a sunny summer.

Plenitude is summer's call,
Varying from the past into a future,
In a surprising survival force.

Who picks such call and follows,
Is a winner with nature,
Not necessarily in our understanding.

But when all Good and Bad
Have found each other,
Summer leaves hope to continue .

(Words, Martin Kari, 2017)

Land besuchen Gras und Felder,
Bäume zeigen, was sie tragen,
Während Wein im Feld wartet.

Auch Menschen lieben die Sonne,
Selbst im Schatten bei der Arbeit,
Freut sich die Sonne mit uns.

Regen sucht Wege in Flüssen,
Auf Geheiß von Mutter Natur,
Dem sonnigen Sommer zu dienen.

Alles vervielfachen heißt Sommer,
Aus Vergangenem für eine Zukunft,
In Kräften für ein Fortleben.

Wer solchem Ruf folgt,
Gewinnt mit der Natur,
Nur bedingt für uns selbst.

Wenn Gut als auch Schlecht,
Sind sich gekommen näher,
Bringt Sommer die Hoffnung weiter.

(Worte, Martin Kari, 2017)

The Hand of Trust

Many hands make much possible ;
And where do these hands come from?
Two hands we can claim our own,
Every other hand should be beneficial
As long as faith accompanies it.
And what does a trust-hand looks like?

A hand usually is visible for us
And what about the hand of trust ?
Has anybody ever seen this hand ?
If not, how come ?
Does the invisible still exists,
When it comes to lending a helping hand ?

All we do, hope, achieve, even fail
Is carried by trust invisibly too,
When answers don't reach us anymore.
All is left, is faith in ourselves,
Trusted to your next of kin, a friend,
Restoring confidence to carry on.

Die Hand des Vertrauens

Viele Hände erreichen viel.
Und woher kommen solche Hände?
Zwei Hände stehen einem jeden von uns zu,
Eine jede Hand mehr sollte hilfreich sein,
Solange jedoch Vertrauen sie begleitet.
Und wie sieht eine vertrauensvolle Hand aus?

Gewöhnlich sind Hände sichtbar,
Wie steht das mit einer Hand des Vertrauens?
Hat jemand solch eine Hand jemals gesehen?
Und wenn nicht, wie kann dies sein?
Ist etwas Unsichtbares dennoch vorhanden?
Besonders wenn es um eine helfende Hand geht?

All unser Tun, Hoffen, Bestreben, selbst Fehlen
Stellen Vertrauen unsichtbar für uns in Frage,
Besonders wenn Antworten ausbleiben.
Dann stellt die Frage des Vertrauens sich uns selbst,
Weiterhin an unsere Nächsten, einen Freund,
Zuversicht suchend, um weiter zu kommen.

Words can become a supporting hand,
They need to be chosen carefully,
Not to disrupt the path to trust.
Action too can support and undermine,
Depending much on a timing,
Where a will finds an open door.

The opponents of a hand of trust
Also rise invisibly from obscurity,
Recruiting lies, deception, fake, fraud,
Which only suppress in a trial of strength
A good will of many a hands,
Including the hand of trust.

No matter what happens, faith is crucial
In any circumstances of a daily life,
Even love depends on the hand of trust,
Because where is no trust, there is no love.
And how much derives from love,
Gives us the understanding of trust.

(Words, Martin Kari – 2016)

Worte können eine hilfreiche Hand unterstützen,
Sofern sie mit Vorsicht walten
Und nicht den Weg zum Vertrauen stören.
Handlung kann sowohl helfen, als auch stören,
Viel entscheidet hier die Zeit,
Wann ein Wille Freiheit erfährt.

Die Gegenspieler der Hand des Vertrauens
Verharren ebenfalls im Schatten,
Sie stützen sich auf Lügen, Täuschung, Betrug,
Welche in einem Aufbegehren
Nur den guten Willen von so mancher Hand
Zunichte machen, einschließlich die des Vertrauens.

Was auch immer geschehen mag, Vertrauen ist wichtig
In allen Umständen des täglichen Lebens.
Selbst Liebe bedarf der Hand des Vertrauens,
Denn wo kein Vertrauen, da ist keine Liebe,
Und wieviel wir der Liebe verdanken,
Gibt die Hand des Vertrauens uns zu verstehen.

(Worte, Martin Kari – 2016)

About Life

At 20 we start living,
Full of delight, ahead we are looking.
From 30 on we set us a goal
Which at 40 we hope to achieve
Until 50 it can last, if it is not lost.
Then quality of life comes in,
Because 60 is ringing in.
Finally time receives its appreciation
And friendship calls for its attention.
Unnoticed the 70-ies turn up,
For wine and peace the thumbs go up.
From the 80-ies beauty pleases us,
Family spoils and pampers us,
The 90-ies gently wait, more silent
And at 100 wisdom is awaiting us.

(Words, Martin Kari 2016)

So Läuft das Leben

Mit 20 fängt man an zu leben
Voll Freude will man vorwärts streben.
Ab 30 steckt man sich ein Ziel,
Das man bis 40 erreichen will.
Mit Energie man vieles schafft
Und noch mit 50 reicht die Kraft;
Jetzt schätzt man Lebensqualität,
Weil es auf die 60 geht.
Genießerisch nützt man die Zeit
Und pflegt auch die Geselligkeit.
Unbemerkt geht's auf die 70 zu.
Man lobt den Wein und schätzt die Ruh,
Ab 80 freut man sich am Schönen,
Läßt von den Seinen sich verwöhnen.
Dann wird man 90 still und leise
Und ab 100 ist man weise.

(Worte, Martin Kari-2016)

Gone are the days

(words: Martin Kari - 2016)

What was, is gone, can we bring it back ?
It still can haunt us in many ways,
Good and less good ones
That we wish it back in eager expectation,
But equally sometimes rejecting it, too.

When things once happened differently,
Was it good or rather bad ?
Why has it changed ?
Changed is said to be a necessity,
Because progress drives our lives.

And what looks good in our eyes ?
Doesn't everybody has his/her own views
How things in life go good or bad
When driven by incident, accident,
Or that time holds its grip on us ?

One time we are exhibiting pride,
But not without a challenge
From the past, present or a future.
Gone by days have adopted distance
Which have rather retreated memories.

```
            P
            R
            E
   PAST     S     FUTURE
            E
            N
            T
```

Was einmal war, ist vorbei !
Können wir es wieder zurückholen ?
Ob gut oder weniger gut?
Einmal wünschen wir es uns sehnsüchtig,
Ein ander Mal verwerfen wir es.

Was zurück liegt war vermeintlich anders,
War es gut, wie nahe war es dem Schlechten ?
Wo hatte es sich eingenistet ?
Änderung soll demgegenüber notwendig sein,
Weil Fortschritt sein Vasall ist.

Und was ist in unseren Augen gut ?
Hat nicht ein Jeder sein eigenes Augenmaß
Für Dinge wie sie gut oder schlecht gehen,
Wenn Zufall, Absicht, Unfall mitspielen,
Oder auch die Zeit ihr Sagen hat ?

Einmal kommt am Ende Stolz heraus,
Jedoch nicht unangefochten einfach
Aus der Vergangenheit, Gegenwart, der Zukunft.
Was vorbei ist, geht gerne auf Distanz,
Es hält Erinnerungen gerne in seinem Bann.

```
                    G
                    E
                    G
                    E
VERGANGENHEIT       N       ZUKUNFT
                    W
                    A
                    R
                    T
```

Memories allowing good to prevail,
Which is the motor for a present,
Because bad got caught in its own game,
With time losing the choice of freedom
To keep us in the present busy.

Comprehension and learning are in demand,
From the past for a future.
And missing building blocks here
Make every foundation shaky
For a future in particular.

And to ease this process,
Memories give good and positive a priority.
How often do we look then back,
Forgiving ourselves and others
In a present brighter light ?

This always maintains fresh impetus
In the present as well as a future,
Supressing an unforeseen sting of the bad,
So that time can heal past wounds
Most of the time quiet but lasting.

Erinnerungen, welche dem Guten Platz gewähren,
Sind der ausschlaggebende Motor der Gegenwart,
Da das Schlechte im eigenen Spiel gefangen ist
Und im Zusammenspiel mit der Zeit
Uns beschäftigt auf Kosten der Freizügigkeit.

Verständigung und Lernen sind dann gefragt,
Aus der Vergangenheit für eine Zukunft.
Ein jeder fehlender Baustein
Gefährdet hier unser Wollen und Können,
Besonders im Hinblick auf eine Zukunft.

Um solchem Bemühen Aufwind zu geben,
Haben gute und positive Erinnerungen Vorrang.
Wie oft blicken wir dabei zurück,
Erlassen uns und anderen Vorwürfe
In einem möglichen besseren Anschein.

Nur Gutes erwacht aus solcher Einstellung,
Sowohl in einer Gegenwart als auch Zukunft,
Der ‚Stachel' des Bösen bleibt so gebannt,
Damit die Zeit Wunden heilen kann,
Meist wenig auffällig in Ruhe, aber nachhaltig.

But overestimation of the past
Also will add to present blindness
Derailing the days of a future
With set impasses from a past
So happiness becomes a distance.

All is good that ends good
And so is it with all three parts,
A past, a present and a future,
When they receive the right attention,
Not too little, not too much.

(Words, Martin Kari 2016)

Überbewertung aus der Vergangenheit
Führt jedoch zu Blindheit in der Gegenwart.
Dies gefährdet die Tage der Zukunft
Einseitig mit seinem Fehlen,
Weshalb auch Freude auf Distanz bleibt.

Am Ende ist doch alles gut, was gut endet.
Und danach streben auch die 3 Epochen,
Die Vergangenheit, die Gegenwart, die Zukunft.
Solange wir notwendige Aufmerksamkeit zollen,
Nicht zu wenig, aber auch nicht zu viel.

(Worte, Martin Kari , 2016)

The Old House

Ghosts gain a foothold anywhere,
As long as it is to their liking,
And the old house across the street
Has prepared itself long enough To become vacant for too long.

The outside paint is visibly peeling off,
Shutters don't do their task anymore,
Thea are either open or halfway shut,
And when wind catches up with them,
They squeak deeply cawing single tones.

The many glass panels allow no clear views,
Its thin curtain linings tell about better times,
While the main entrance door stays shut.
No motor vehicle adds to a pride of the house,
The clothes line waits abandoned empty.

Weeds have suppressed the grass in height,
Only here and there shines little colour
From a long bygone garden with flowers,
While wooden slats along the road front
Barely can stand up with gaps and a crooked gate.

Das Alte Haus

Gespenster haben ein zu Hause dort,
Wo auch ihre Welt einen Platz bekommt,
So hat das alte Haus gegenüber
Lange genug sich so zurück gezogen,
Daß es schon lange unbewohnt geblieben ist.

Seine Fassadenfarbe blättert schon sichtbar ab,
Fensterläden erfüllen ihre Aufgabe nicht mehr,
Sie verweilen offen oder halb geschlossen,
Und wenn der Wind zu ihnen kommt,
Antworten sie tief krächzend.

Die kleinen Glasfelder sind nicht mehr klar,
Vorhangstränge erzählen von besseren Zeiten,
Während die Haupt Eingangstüre zu bleibt,
Gibt auch kein Fahrzeug Stolz dem Haus,
Selbst die Wäschespinne wartet einsam leer.

Unkraut hat das Gras bereits überwuchert,
Nur stellenweise leuchtet noch Farbe
Aus einem lang vergangenen Blumengarten.
Die Zaunlatten entlang der Straße
Widerstehen den Lücken, dem schiefen Tor.

Although the roof top appears immaculate,
Its colour stand out in a grey-greenly tone
And how would the house-inside look like ?
Even from another hidden door in its back,
Which raises suspicion with its obvious bullet holes.

Kids from the nearby school have found out already
This door is closed but not locked at all,
Inviting after school-hours some youngsters
Regularly to play up inside the old house,
Banishing the silence for a short while.

Be it now the time for youngsters or ghosts,
Together to escape from school and home,
With hide and seek run around in empty rooms,
Which daylight mixed with shadows from outside,
Challenge the youngsters early too easy understanding.

Gaping void still fills the old house interior,
So much the more when freedom returns,
After uninvited visitors have left again,
Leaving behind the trail for ghosts,
So the old house continues its vacancy in silence.

(Words, Martin Kari-2016)

All dem zum Trotz erscheint das Dach gut,
Seine grau-grüne Farbe sticht jedoch hervor,
Und wie mag wohl das Haus innen aussehen?
Selbst mit einem Zugang von hinten versteckt,
Wo bereits Schusslöcher Zweifel anmelden.

Kinder der nahen Schule fanden bereits heraus,
Diese Türe bleibt niemals verschlossen.
So lädt sie nach der Schule ein,
Zu Fangspielen im alten Haus,
Seine Stille für kurze Zeit zu verbannen.

Dies ist die Zeit für Kinder und Gespenster,
Der Schule und dem zu Hause zu entgehen,
Mit Versteckspielen durch die leeren Zimmer,
Nur im Licht von außen, gemischt mit Schatten
Ist der Kinderspaß getestet.

Völlige Stille kehrt in das alte Haus zurück,
Sobald Frieden wieder Einzug gehalten hat,
Die nicht geladenen Besucher gegangen sind,
Spuren lediglich der Geister zurück bleiben,
So fährt das alte Haus fort mit seiner Leere.

(Worte, Martin Kari-2016)

Christmas

(Words, Martin Kari, 2016)

Christmas again has arrived,
A whole year has it taken,
Throughout many orders and nights,
The day battling the nights,
To show us its light,
Where Good and Bad find common ground.

A past is then easier forgotten,
Something new casts its spell,
With joy, hope and confidence,
With joy, because sorrow has to give way,
While hope gives the new direction,
And confidence helps to preserve so much.

Doors are then here to remain open,
Hearts openly meat others,
A present facilitates something thought difficult,
With calm and piece in a light,
Which nature accompanies
Right into our home.

Weihnachten

(Worte , Martin Kari-2016)

Ein ganzes Jahr hat es gedauert,
Durch viele Weihen und Nächte hindurch,
Hat der Tag mit der Nacht gerungen,
Das Licht des Lebens Weihnachten steht wieder vor der Tür,uns zu zeigen,
Wo Gutes und Böses sich vereinen.

Was war, wird dann leichter vergessen,
Das Neue hält uns im Banne,
Mit Freude, Hoffnung und Zuversicht,
Mit Freude, weil Leid zurücktreten muß,
Hoffnung gibt uns die neue Richtung,
Während Zuversicht hilft so vieles zu erhalten.

Türen sollten jetzt offen sein,
Herzen zueinander finden,
Ein Geschenk den Nächsten erreichen,
Mit Ruhe und Frieden im Lichtschein,
Den wir uns mit der Natur
In unser Heim gebracht haben.

Shines into many a heart,
Carried by words, too,
Even against much a will,
Including wonderful music,
When peace allows a guess,
What the world could be like.

Differences stay, differences go,
What remains is our will,
To follow the call for freedom,
To appease others,
Forget about worthlessness,
To give a new beginning a start.

Who stays in the middle of life,
Is challenged without question,
Because here decisions are made,
Whether or not a Christmas,
Is stimulated by us,
Back to its destination.

Leuchtend in viele Herzen,
Von Worten getragen,
Auch gegen so manchen Willen,
Bis hin zu wunderbarer Musik,
Läßt solcher Frieden einzig ahnen,
Wie diese Welt sein könnte.

Unterschiede bleiben, Unterschiede gehen,
Was uns prägt, ist unser Wille,
Dem Ruf nach Frieden zu folgen,
Versöhnlich den Anderen stimmen,
Vergessen, was nicht wert ist.
Einem Neubeginn das Tor wieder öffnen.

Wer in des Lebens Mitte steht,
Bleibt nicht unangefochten,
Denn auch hier fällt die Entscheidung,
Ob, ob nicht ein Weihnachten,
Neu belebt durch uns,
Zurück zu seiner Bestimmung findet.

Religion is Poesy, Too

'Religio' says, I believe,
It does raise hope,
Likewise first a flower,
Displaying beauty,
For the one who comprehends,
To deal with beauty, too.

Here challenge only adds to conviction,
Nobody is spared from it,
The one discovers with poesy,
Voices giving answers,
Others are kept imprisoned by haste,
Barred from winning over a belief.

Nobody however is perfect,
And poesy shows only directions, too,
In a belief just as off-side,
Finding back to the essentials,
To keep us going,
Even past our time-limits.

(Words, Martin Kari – 2017)

Religion & Poesie

Religio sagt, ich glaube,
Sie gibt Halt im Leben,
Gleich einer Blume,
Entfaltet es sich zum Schönen,
Für den, der versteht,
Auch mit Schönem umzugehen.

Anfechtung stärkt hier Überzeugung,
Keinem bleibt dies erspart,
Der Eine hört im Poesie-Klang
Stimmen mit Antworten,
Andere bannt die Eile,
Einsicht im Glauben zu gewinnen.

Niemand ist jedoch erhaben,
Denn Poesie weist Wege,
Im Glauben wie im Abseits,
Zurück zu finden zum Wesentlichen,
Was uns erhalten kann,
Über eine Zeit hinaus.

———❈———

(Worte, Martin Kari, 2017)

www.ingramcontent.com/pod-product-compliance
Lightning Source LLC
Chambersburg PA
CBHW030555080526
44585CB00012B/385